UNDERSTANDIN~
THE STORY
THE OLD TE~

HOPE

FOR ALL THE EARTH

MITCHELL L. CHASE

Copyright © 2022 by Mitchell L. Chase

First published in Great Britain in 2022

The right of Mitchell L. Chase to be identified as the Author of this Work has been asserted by him in accordance with the Copyright, Designs and Patents Act 1988.

British Library Cataloguing in Publication Data
A record for this book is available from the British Library

ISBN: 978-1-913896-85-0

Designed and typeset by Pete Barnsley (CreativeHoot.com)

Printed in Denmark

10Publishing, a division of 10ofthose.com
Unit C, Tomlinson Road, Leyland, PR25 2DY, England

Email: info@10ofthose.com
Website: www.10ofthose.com

1 3 5 7 10 8 6 4 2

For Jensen, Logan, Owen, and Grayson,
my four beloved sons.

May your hearts rejoice in Christ,
the hope of all the earth.

CONTENTS

A SELECT TIMELINE

The following list of dates is a timeline of major Old Testament events.

2000 BC	The call of, and covenant with, Abraham
1446 BC	The exodus of the Israelites out of Egypt under Moses
1446–1406 BC	The forty years of wandering
1406 BC	The conquest of the promised land under Joshua
1010 BC	The beginning of David's reign
970–930 BC	The reign of Solomon
930 BC	The division of Israel's united kingdom

722 BC	The destruction of the northern kingdom by Assyria
586 BC	The destruction and exile of the southern kingdom by Babylon
539 BC	The end of the Babylonian captivity
536 BC	The return of many exiles to the promised land
520 BC	The ministries of Haggai and Zechariah
516 BC	The completion of the rebuilt temple
483–473 BC	The story of the book of Esther
458 BC	The arrival of Ezra
444 BC	The completion of the rebuilt wall around Jerusalem under Nehemiah

INTRODUCTION:

THE BIBLE JESUS READ

The Old Testament exists to prepare the way for the Lord Jesus Christ. The narratives and songs, the prophecies and patterns, point to the Savior who would rescue us from our sin and establish an everlasting kingdom. Jesus is the hope for all the earth.

These thirty-nine Old Testament books are the Bible that Jesus read. Joseph and Mary would have taught him the Scriptures as he grew, and he would have delighted in its divine commands. Jesus treasured the Old Testament, and at the same time he was—and is—its treasure. The many characters and promises and institutions in these books were like shadowy outlines of the coming Christ.

As Jesus read the ancient words of the faith, he would have discerned in the Scriptures that he was the covenant Son, the true Israel, the promised king, the greater temple, and the perfect priest. While such ideas will become clearer as our study of the Old Testament unfolds, Jesus knew he was fulfilling expectations and patterns that dated back millennia.

After Jesus' resurrection, he told his disciples, "This is what I told you while I was still with you: Everything must be fulfilled that is written about me in the Law of Moses, the Prophets and the Psalms" (Luke 24:44). The Scriptures which Jesus read had testified of him.

We need the New Testament to understand the Old, and we need the Old Testament to understand the New. But haven't you sensed how much more challenging the Old Testament is to read and interpret? The Old Testament makes up three-quarters of our Bibles, so we would be wise to study it and think through the Big Picture.

The Old Testament was written over a period of one thousand years. More than thirty authors were involved in the composition of its thirty-nine books. Paul wrote, "All Scripture is God-breathed and is useful for teaching, rebuking, correcting and training in righteousness" (2 Tim. 3:16). The Holy Spirit inspired the biblical authors, ensuring that the content of the Old Testament is true and trustworthy.

The more we understand the Old Testament story, the more we can rejoice in Christ together, since the biblical authors anticipated his advent. Their message of hope was not just for some parts of the world. News of a coming Savior should be spread as far and wide as the reach of sin and death.

Do you see Christ in the Old Testament? Do you want to recognize the ways it points to him? The reason Jesus saw himself in Scripture was because of its design. The Bible Jesus read was a Bible about Jesus. As we understand the Old Testament in light of its grand purpose, we shall be blessed readers indeed. Let's learn more about Holy Scripture, then, pursuing greater joy in Jesus.

IN AND OUT OF SACRED SPACE

In the beginning, God created the heavens and the earth so that we might glorify him and enjoy him forever. He formed and filled creation, making it habitable for creatures and particularly his image bearers (Gen. 1:26–27). All the work God did was through his Son, the Word, who was with him in the beginning before the foundation of the world (John 1:1–3). By the Son all things hold together, and for him all things exist (Col. 1:16–17).

We live in a universe made for the glory of Jesus Christ, and we read a Bible written for that same purpose. We need to understand how the foundation of our faith begins in Genesis.

CREATED AND COMMISSIONED

Adam and Eve were our first parents, whom God made by his power and in his image. They dwelled in sacred space, a garden in Eden, and there God blessed them with abundance and life. This space was sacred because the conditions outside Eden weren't the same as those inside Eden. This place was set apart as ground zero for a global, glory-spreading project. As image bearers, Adam and Eve represented God in creation, tasked with subduing and exercising dominion over the land as they became fruitful and multiplied (Gen. 1:26–28).

Like a king's image represents his authority and claim over that territory, God's image bearers represented him in the world he had made. God was the cosmic king, and Adam and Eve were his viceregents; they were king and queen of creation who were to bring honor to the one they represented.

If Adam and Eve would have remained in the Garden of Eden, no doubt the boundaries of that sacred space would have expanded to include their descendants: image bearers whose lives would glorify the Lord with worship and obedience. The expansion of the garden would be in sync with the goal of God's creative acts: to fill the earth "with the knowledge of the glory of the LORD as the waters cover the sea" (Hab. 2:14).

But Adam and Eve did not remain.

TAKING WHAT IS FORBIDDEN

In the center of the garden were two trees: the tree of life and the tree of the knowledge of good and evil. God gave a command concerning the second tree: "You are free to eat from any tree in the garden; but you must not eat from the tree of the knowledge of good and evil, for when you eat from it you will certainly die" (Gen. 2:16–17).

Isn't it easy to focus on what is forbidden so that we fail to grasp the vastness of God's gracious provision? The allure of what is forbidden can be strong. You can wonder if God is holding out on you, whether he really loves you, whether he's really as good as the Scripture claims.

Into the sacred space of Eden there came a tempter. The crafty serpent came to the woman and bent God's words (Gen. 3:1–5). The tempter depicted God as stingy and misleading. In fact, he directly contradicted God's warning by saying, "You will not certainly die" (3:4).

Rather than trusting and submitting to God's wisdom, Eve took and ate the desirable fruit (Gen. 3:6). Her husband, who was with her, took it next and ate as well.

God had given Adam the responsibility to work and keep the garden (Gen. 2:15). These would be the same roles of the future Israelite priests who served and guarded the sacred space of the tabernacle (Num. 3:7–8). Foreshadowing these priests, Adam failed in his task. He did not guard the garden; he did not preserve its holiness faithfully. By heeding the tempter's words, Adam and Eve disregarded God's command and defiled his sacred space.

Great was their fall, for in them we fell as well. Sin came into the world through one man, and death through sin (Rom. 5:12).

THE IDEA TO HIDE FROM GOD

Transgression brought alienation. Adam and Eve planned to hide from the all-seeing God, feeling shame and guilt for what they had done. They tried to cover up their own nakedness, as if their efforts could compensate for rebellion against the God who is light and life.

Even though they were physically alive, the dynamics of death were already working within them. Sin wants to conceal, to move into darker places where judgment won't reach. How foolish sin is, then, for nothing can be hidden from the God who knows all. There is nowhere he is not.

The Lord called to Adam and Eve and asked about their decision, but they only blame-shifted, evading responsibility by pointing to another (Gen. 3:8–13). Sin brings disorder and damages relationships—both our relationship with God and our relationships with others.

We need restoration from the alienation of sin. We need atonement, but this is not a covering we can configure for ourselves. We learn from the story of Adam and Eve that only God can bring us back to God.

SALVATION THROUGH JUDGMENT

God is holy, so he must judge sin. Would he be worthy of worship if he showed unrighteous indifference in the face of rebellion and wickedness? The Lord who made Adam and Eve spoke words of judgment, first to the serpent, then to the woman, and then to the man (Gen. 3:14–19).

Working backward from that order, we read that Adam learned about the toilsome work that would be his lot. The ground would be cursed (Gen. 3:17), and death would bring his body—and ours—back to that ground (3:19). The cursed dust would consume our life.

Eve learned that both childbearing and marriage would be affected (Gen. 3:16). She would experience pains she wouldn't want as well as desires she shouldn't have. Nevertheless, there is language about bringing forth children, so the commission to be "fruitful and increase in number" (1:28) would continue in a fallen world.

To the serpent God spoke about a future son of Eve, and this promise is the fountain of hope for a deliverer: "And I will put enmity between you and the woman, and between your offspring and hers; he will crush your head, and you will strike his heel" (Gen. 3:15).

When we look carefully at God's words to the serpent, there is a promise of judgment and of victory. The serpent will be judged ("he will crush your head"), but the future son's victory will be through suffering ("you will strike his heel").

If the actions of the first Adam brought such devastation through transgression, there is hope that this future son—a better Adam—might accomplish what would reverse the curse. If rebellion brought alienation, guilt, and death, salvation must bring reconciliation, forgiveness, and resurrection.

This promised descendant of Eve—the future offspring of the woman—is Jesus of Nazareth, sent from God and born of Mary.

EAST OF EDEN

The Lord clothed Adam and Eve with garments of skins (Gen. 3:21). This provision surpassed their feeble attempts at covering themselves, and it foreshadowed the importance to Israel of animal offerings being given in the place of sinners. God would shed blood to bring atonement. Ultimately Jesus himself would give his life so that we might be clothed in his righteousness.

The confrontational scene in Genesis 3 ends with exile. Adam and Eve, and everyone after them, would live outside Eden. God placed cherubim and a flaming sword that guarded the entrance at the east of the garden (Gen. 3:24).

Now exiled from sacred space, Adam and Eve would spend the remainder of their days in a world marked by the effects of sin and death. They were separated from the tree of life (Gen. 3:22), and therefore would surely die. But first they would be fruitful and multiply.

SEED OF THE WOMAN AND OF THE SERPENT

Cain and Abel were born to Adam and Eve. These brothers were the first examples of the seed of the woman and the seed of the serpent, which are the spiritual categories that apply to all the human descendants of Adam and Eve. Those who hope in the Lord are the seed of the woman, and those who turn from the Lord are the seed of the serpent.

Cain's spiritual condition was clear by his murder of Abel (Gen. 4:8), but the birth of Seth renewed hope for the line of promise (4:25–26). This line is traced through Genesis 5. We learn that Noah's father Lamech named him Noah hoping that "He will comfort us in the labor and painful toil of our hands caused by the ground the LORD has cursed" (5:29).

Lamech longed for a promised deliverer, and he hoped his son would be the one. While Noah wasn't the one who would overcome the serpent, he played a major role in the flood sent by God (Gen. 6–8). God determined to judge the pervasive and unceasing wickedness of mankind (6:5). But he delivered Noah and Noah's family from a watery judgment by securing them in an ark.

After the flood, Noah was a new Adam with the same commission (see Gen. 1:28; 9:1). God confirmed his covenant with Noah and with Noah's family and with all creatures on the earth (9:8–11). A covenant in Scripture is a formal relationship and agreement. With covenantal language, God promised never to flood the earth again.

As Noah's family expanded, the spiritual identities of the seed of the woman and the seed of the serpent were present as well (Gen. 9–11). Nations and languages developed and spread, all in a fallen world that needed the mercy of God.

The ground was cursed, and image bearers were sinful. Could there be future blessing that would make a difference?

EXPECTING JESUS

- Jesus is the Son of God by whom and for whom all things exist.

- Jesus is the promised Seed of the woman who would defeat the serpent and overcome the curse.

- Jesus is the Last Adam whose sinless life and obedience would bring the hope of salvation to sinners.

- The death of Jesus accomplished full and final atonement so that sinners could be reconciled to God through him.

SUGGESTED READING

- Genesis 1–9
- Matthew 4:1–11
- Romans 5:12–21
- Colossians 1:15–20

2

A FAMILY THAT BECOMES A NATION

God set apart a family to save the world. Around 2000 BC, the Lord called a man named Abraham to leave behind his home and ancestors and to enter a promised land (Gen. 12:1–9). This destination—known then as Canaan—would be the place of Abraham's descendants.

It is hard to underestimate the importance of this land. The Israelites would inherit it centuries later, the city of Jerusalem would be there, and the Lord Jesus would be born, minister, die, and rise there.

A COVENANT AND SIGN

The promised seed of the woman would be born from the family of Abraham (Gen. 3:15;

12:7; Gal. 3:16). The most immediate obstacle to God fulfilling his promises to the patriarch was that Abraham's wife, Sarah, was barren (Gen. 11:30). But Abraham—and the readers of the Old Testament—saw God repeatedly prove that he has the power to back up his promises.

Abraham learned that he and Sarah would have a son (Gen. 15:4; 17:17). In fact, when all is said and done with God's purposes, the offspring of Abraham will be as numerous as the uncountable stars (15:5; Rev. 7:9).

God promised Abraham seed and land (Gen. 12:2; 13:14–17), and he made these promises as a covenant (15:18). The sign of circumcision represented the setting apart of Abraham and his descendants (17:9–14). Since the act of circumcision was external, there was still a necessity for Hebrew children to follow God from the heart. External circumcision would not guarantee an inward devotion to God; a circumcision of the heart was vital. We learn later that this was something only God could do (Rom. 2:28–29).

FROM ABRAHAM TO ISAAC

In the fullness of time, God brought to pass the promise of a son for Abraham. When Sarah gave birth to Isaac, she was ninety years old, and Abraham was one hundred. The promised line would continue through Isaac, for the Lord said to Abraham that "it is through Isaac that your offspring will be reckoned" (Gen. 21:12).

When Isaac was a young man, the Lord tested Abraham and told him to offer Isaac on a mountain in the land of Moriah (Gen. 22:1–2). We see Abraham's faith and obedience as he led Isaac—and a couple of servants—to the appointed region and mountain. Abraham told the men, "Stay here with the donkey while I and the boy go over there. We will worship and then we will come back to you" (22:5). Abraham anticipated returning with Isaac alive because he believed God would raise his son from the dead (Heb. 11:17–19).

In what seemed to be the last moments of Isaac's life, an angel intervened (Gen. 22:11–12). Abraham offered a ram instead, calling the place "The LORD Will Provide" (22:14). This animal substitute foreshadowed the sacrificial offerings that would be integral to Israel's way of life. Solomon later built the temple in Jerusalem "on Mount Moriah" (2 Chr. 3:1), where Abraham had once offered up his son Isaac. Many years after that, the Lord Jesus would lay down his own life as the son of Abraham and Son of God. Jesus was the true and greater Isaac. Through the atoning sacrifice of the perfect promised Son, the Lord would provide.

FROM ISAAC TO JACOB

Isaac married Rebekah, and she too faced barrenness (Gen. 25:21). As God did for Sarah, he opened the womb of Rebekah. She gave birth to Jacob and Esau, and learned that these two sons represented two nations who would come from them (25:23). God blessed Isaac with the language reminiscent of his father Abraham: "I am the God of your father Abraham. Do not be afraid, for I am with you; I will bless you and will increase the number of your descendants for the sake of my servant Abraham" (26:24).

But there was conflict and tension between Jacob and Esau during their lives, and Jacob fled to his Uncle Laban's home in Paddan Aram for many years. While on the way, the Lord told him,

I am the Lord, the God of your father Abraham and the God of Isaac. I will give you and your descendants the land on which you are lying. Your descendants will be like the dust of the earth, and you will spread out to the west and to the east, to the north and to the south. All peoples on earth will be blessed through you and your offspring (Gen. 28:13–14).

God's covenant with Abraham was the same for Isaac and then the same for Jacob. The stories of the patriarchs reveal a continuity in God's promises.

FROM JACOB TO TWELVE SONS

The descendants of Abraham continued to multiply as Jacob married Leah, Rachel, and their respective maidservants (Gen. 29–30). Through these women Jacob had twelve sons, and these sons would become heads of the tribes which bore their names. The number of these sons explains why Jesus chose twelve disciples. He was establishing a new Israel, right in the midst of the promised land.

Why was the nation called Israel? Because of a name change. The Lord told Jacob, "Your name will no longer be Jacob, but Israel, because you have struggled with God and with humans and have overcome" (Gen. 32:28). Jacob's descendants are known as the Israelites because they are the children of Israel (Jacob).

One of Jacob's twelve sons was Joseph, and Joseph had dreams that he would be in authority and rule over his family (Gen. 37:1–11). Joseph's brothers were jealous of him and irritated by his dreams. When an opportunity came to rid themselves of Joseph, they seized the moment. They sold him to some Ishmaelites (37:28) and deceived their father Jacob with a torn and bloody robe. Jacob said, "It is my son's robe! Some ferocious animal has devoured him. Joseph has surely been torn to pieces" (37:33).

Joseph was sold to the house of Potiphar in Egypt. But what the brothers meant for evil, God meant for good.

FROM CANAAN TO EGYPT

Joseph was faithful to the Lord in a foreign land. Though this faithfulness cost him his reputation and freedom, the Lord was with him (Gen. 39:23). When Joseph correctly interpreted the dreams of his fellow prisoners, the Pharaoh eventually learned of this ability and called for him (41:14).

The Pharaoh had dreams that needed explanation, and Joseph provided it: there would be seven years of plenty, followed by seven years of famine, in the land of Egypt and elsewhere (Gen. 41:25–36). The vindication of Joseph had come. Pharaoh appointed him over all the land (41:41–44). From this position in the Egyptian administration, Joseph would ensure the survival of Egypt and of anyone who traveled there to him from the promised land.

One day Joseph's brothers—minus Benjamin—arrived in his presence needing food (Gen. 42:6). He recognized them, but they didn't recognize him. He learned his father Jacob was still alive. Joseph's knowledge of them allowed him some time to try various schemes to get Benjamin to join them in Egypt, since Benjamin was his only brother from his mother Rachel. Unable to bear the ruse any longer though, Joseph made himself known and experienced a moving reunion with his siblings who had formerly tried to exile him (45:1–15).

The next step was transferring Jacob and the rest of the family to Egypt. After they had begun their journey, Joseph reunited with his father at last (Gen. 46:29). With Pharaoh's blessing, the Israelites would dwell in a region of Egypt known as Goshen, and there they would thrive instead of perishing in a famine.

A SCEPTER AND JUDAH'S TRIBE

Near the end of Jacob's life, he called his sons so he might bless them. To Judah, his fourth-born son, he said, "The scepter will not depart from Judah, nor the ruler's staff from between his feet, until he to whom it belongs shall come and the obedience of the nations shall be his" (Gen. 49:10).

A scepter, or "ruler's staff," is what a king would have, associating royalty with Judah's tribe. The individual who would receive obedience is the same person as the Genesis 3:15 son. The reader can have hope that a future deliverer will arise from Judah's tribe to overcome the serpent and reverse the effects of the curse, and that this rescuer will be royal.

Jacob's words to Judah point beyond those days to the days of Jesus, who was from Judah's tribe. To Jesus belongs the obedience of the nations, and his name is worth tribute and praise.

EXPECTING JESUS

- Jesus, the Seed of the woman, descended from the family of Abraham.

- As a true and greater Isaac, Jesus is the heir of God's promises.

- Jesus is the true Israel who gathered twelve disciples.

- Jesus is the royal one from Judah's tribe, from whom the scepter will never depart.

SUGGESTED READING

- Genesis 12–17
- Genesis 25–50
- Matthew 1:1–17
- Galatians 3:7–14

3

FROM EGYPT TO THE PROMISED LAND

As generations passed in the land of Goshen, the Israelites became enslaved by a fearful Pharaoh who felt threatened by their increasing numbers (Ex. 1:8–14). And the Lord raised up Moses to deliver them.

The introduction of Moses comes when he was a child (Ex. 2:1–10). Divine providence placed him in the household of Pharaoh until Moses was forty years old, and he lived the next forty years in the land of Midian, where he married and started a family. At eighty years old, Moses encountered the Lord's voice when he saw a bush on fire (3:1–6; Acts 7:23, 29–30).

THE MISSION FOR MOSES

On Mount Horeb—also known as Mount Sinai—Moses heard about his mission to lead the Israelites out of Egypt. The Israelites were the corporate son of God (Ex. 4:22). And through mighty signs and wonders, God would bring his son out of captivity for the purpose of worshipping him. He would redeem the Israelites. Their journey would be from Egypt to the promised land (3:8).

The Israelites were initially receptive to Moses, though the rising ruthlessness of Pharaoh embittered them (Ex. 4–5). Moses' appearances before the Egyptian king didn't appear effective—yet all of this was according to what the Lord had spoken.

Moses' mission was impossible for him to complete, and that was the point. God would act by a mighty hand and outstretched arm. God could do what was impossible for Moses.

THE MIGHTY EXODUS

An outpouring of plagues devastated the land of Egypt. The plagues were each associated with different Egyptian gods, showing Yahweh's[1] power over the idols of the land (Ex. 12:12; Num. 33:4). The tenth plague was the death of the firstborn, when judgment passed through the land of Egypt but passed over the homes of the Israelites if those dwellings were covered by the blood of a slain lamb.

At the death of the firstborn in Egypt, Pharaoh told Moses, "Up! Leave my people, you and the Israelites! Go, worship the LORD as you have requested" (Ex. 12:31). So in approximately 1446 BC, Moses led the Israelites out of slavery. The exodus had begun. Each subsequent year the Israelites were to remember what the Lord had done by having a Feast of Passover and Unleavened Bread. They would collectively recall how God redeemed them for the glory of his name.

The event of the exodus is a vital template for understanding Jesus' ministry. Jesus was the ultimate Passover lamb that provided refuge for those covered by his blood (John 1:29; 1 Cor. 5:7). He died on Passover, fulfilling this feast

---

1   Yahweh is the Hebrew name for God used in the Old Testament.

that had been established fifteen hundred years earlier (Matt. 26:1–2; John 19:14). According to Luke 9:31, Jesus would accomplish a departure, or exodus, at Jerusalem.

THROUGH THE SEA

Coming against the Red Sea, the Israelites feared for their lives. But the Lord once more showed his supremacy and power by parting the waters like walls so that the people could cross on dry ground (Ex. 14:21–22). The Egyptians pursued the people, yet the Lord closed the waters upon the soldiers in judgment (14:26–28).

The deliverance of the Israelites and the judgment on their enemies became a major source of praise in later songs (for example, see Ps. 78:12–13). God was the God of the exodus and the Red Sea deliverance. The gods of Egypt could do nothing, for they were no gods at all. The God of the exodus was the God of heaven and earth, of life and death.

During the exodus, God's mighty hand and outstretched arm accomplished salvation. And in the story line of Scripture, the exodus anticipated the greater work which Jesus would accomplish. On the cross, Jesus' mighty hands and outstretched arms accomplished salvation for sinners. As our greater Moses and perfect Savior, Jesus would lead us through the walls of God's judgment.

A COVENANT AT SINAI

Safe on the other side of the Red Sea, the people pressed on toward Mount Sinai, and along the way God provided for them (Ex. 16–17). He was demonstrating his trustworthiness and faithfulness. The God of Moses was the God of Abraham, Isaac, and Jacob, and that meant he was a God of steadfast love.

Weeks after their exodus in 1446 BC, the Israelites arrived at Mount Sinai. The Lord descended on the mountain in glory and majesty, revealing commandments for his redeemed people (Ex. 19–20). Moses ascended the mountain to receive further instruction and then conveyed it to the people (Ex. 21–23). God's words were holy, righteous, wise, and good.

Having heard what God commanded, the Israelites said, "Everything the LORD has said we will do" (Ex. 24:3). The Lord entered into a covenant with the Israelites. They would be his people, and he would be their God. When they came to the promised land, they would not live like the nations. They would be a light to the nations.

Yet tragedy struck at Sinai. The Israelites had not even left the mountain before they violated the covenant. They fashioned a golden calf while Moses was away, and they proclaimed that it had delivered them from Egypt (Ex. 32:1–8). A plague broke out against the people (32:35). This divine judgment didn't destroy them, however.

The Israelites were learning by experience the truth of what God revealed to Moses in Exodus 34:6–7: "The LORD, the LORD, the compassionate and gracious God, slow to anger, abounding in love and faithfulness, maintaining love to thousands, and forgiving wickedness, rebellion and sin. Yet he does not leave the guilty unpunished; he punishes the children and their children for the sin of the parents to the third and fourth generation."

THE TABERNACLE

During the eleven months that the Israelites dwelled in the wilderness of Sinai, the Lord instructed them to build a portable tent that would serve as a dwelling place for his manifest glory and presence. This portable place was known as the tabernacle.

The tabernacle had a large room called the Holy Place, and it had a smaller cubed room called the Most Holy Place. These two rooms were separated by a veil. The tabernacle was surrounded by a courtyard, and the entrances to both the courtyard and the tabernacle were at the eastern side.

An eastern entrance is a deliberate callback to the Garden of Eden, for cherubim had guarded the eastern entrance after the exile of Adam and Eve (Gen. 3:22–24). Going into the tabernacle symbolized the return to Eden.

The Israelites were also instructed about what the tabernacle was to include. It was to have various pieces of furniture inside (an ark, an altar for incense, a lampstand, and a table for bread), as well as furniture outside that stood in the courtyard itself (a basin of water and an altar for sacrifice).

Through the tabernacle system, the Lord was teaching the Israelites how to approach him. He is holy, worthy, and exalted. The Israelites would therefore approach him through offerings that were given on their behalf, and there would be a group of priests who mediated for them and presented these offerings to God.

The Israelites could approach their holy God through an appropriate substitute. These animal offerings were shadows of the Savior who would come to be the final sacrifice and perfect substitute. The Son of God would tabernacle (dwell) among sinners. In the ministry of Jesus, the grace, blessing, power, and glory of God would bring renewal and reconciliation. The flesh of Jesus would become a new veil, to be torn at the proper time.

AARON AND HIS SONS

Moses' older brother Aaron would serve as Israel's high priest. On one day a year—called the Day of Atonement—he would represent all Israel as he went behind the veil into the Most Holy Place, where he sprinkled blood (Lev. 16).

During the weeks of Israel's calendar, Aaron and the other priests would maintain the functions and furniture of the tabernacle, and their work included the important responsibilities of offering the various sacrifices that the Lord described (Lev. 1–7). They would serve and guard the tabernacle, like Adam was supposed to serve and guard the Garden of Eden (Gen. 2:15).

The tabernacle and the priesthood were signs of God's reconciling grace. Sinners need atonement, and these institutions showed God to be merciful and gracious, slow to anger and abounding in steadfast love (Ex. 34:6–7). And if there was hope for the Israelites, there was hope for the nations. There was hope for the earth.

FORTY YEARS OF WANDERING

The many laws in Exodus and Leviticus revealed how the Israelites were to love God and neighbor. The covenant people departed Mount Sinai for the promised land, where they would live out their devotion to God among the nations who needed to know God.

But not all was well within the hearts of the Israelites. After departing Mount Sinai, many people murmured against the Lord and opposed Moses (Num. 11–12). The worst was yet to come.

As the Israelites neared the promised land, Moses sent ahead a group of spies to examine the land and report back. Forty days later, the spies returned but brought, overall, a bad report

(Num. 13:25–33). In response, the Israelites wept and wailed, grumbling against Moses and against the Lord (14:1–4). People spoke of appointing a new leader and going back to Egypt!

Since the older generation of Israelites was filled with wickedness and unbelief, the Lord pronounced a forty-year judgment (Num. 14:34). During these four decades, the Israelites would wander in the wilderness as people perished. At the end of forty years, the younger generation would have grown up and would be ready to inherit the promised land.

THE ORACLES OF BALAAM

Near the end of the forty years of wandering, the Israelites arrived east of the Jordan River in the plains of Moab (Num. 22:1). The king of Moab, whose name was Balak, asked Balaam (a prophet) to curse the Israelites. Yet when Balaam issued his oracles, he could only bless the people (23:11–12).

Balaam's final oracle included a prophecy about the future son who would rise to reign: "I see him, but not now; I behold him, but not near. A star will come out of Jacob; a scepter will rise out of Israel. He will crush the foreheads of Moab, the skulls of all the people of Sheth" (Num. 24:17).

Balaam prophesied about a future head-crushing rescuer who would descend from the Israelites and reign as a king. Israel's "scepter" recalls the promise from Genesis 49:10, and a skull-crusher recalls Genesis 3:15—the fountainhead of messianic hope. Balaam's prophecy was fulfilled through the life, death, and resurrection of King Jesus.

THE DEATH OF MOSES

In the plains of Moab, Moses reminded the Israelites of their history and of God's laws. He called the people to heed God's commands so that they would be blessed, lest they turn from God's ways and face judgment (Deut. 28). Moses set before them, essentially, life and death. He learned that another prophet like him would arise in the future, a prophet whose words would be the very words of God (18:15–18). Jesus is the prophet like Moses (Acts 3:22–26).

Across from the promised land, Moses died at 120 years old. Among the wilderness generation that would perish before the Israelites inherited the land, perhaps Moses' body was among the last to fall. Now Joshua, the new Moses, would lead the covenant people.

EXPECTING JESUS

- Jesus accomplished a new and greater exodus through his death and resurrection.

- Jesus is the Passover lamb whose blood shields sinners who come to him by faith.

- In his Son's coming to earth, God was tabernacling among sinners, drawing near to them in grace, blessing, power, and glory.

- As the prophet whom Moses foretold, Jesus speaks the words of God which should be believed and obeyed.

SUGGESTED READING

- Exodus 1–15
- Numbers 13–14
- 2 Corinthians 3:1–4:6
- Hebrews 9

4

THE KINGDOM'S RISE AND DEMISE

After being away from the promised land for centuries (see Gen. 46), the Israelites returned to that sacred space where the patriarchs had dwelt. The Lord said to Joshua, "Be strong and very courageous. Be careful to obey all the law my servant Moses gave you; do not turn from it to the right or to the left, that you may be successful wherever you go" (Josh. 1:7).

TAKING THE LAND

If the Israelites left Egypt in 1446 BC, and this was followed by forty years of wilderness wandering, then the conquest of the land began in approximately 1406 BC.

The Lord parted the Jordan River so that the Israelites could enter the land (Josh. 3:14–17), a miracle reminiscent of the Red Sea crossing. Both deliverance and inheritance, therefore, were linked to a miraculous water crossing.

The Israelites conquered kings in southern and northern Canaan (Josh. 10–11). And the tribes of Israel received their various allotments (13–22). Joshua charged the people to serve the Lord (24:22–23). They renewed their covenant to keep God's commands.

The occupation of the promised land showed God's faithfulness to his promise to Abraham. He had promised that "your descendants will come back here" (Gen. 15:16), and under Joshua they did.

Inheriting the promised land not only recalled the Abrahamic covenant; it also echoed the sacred space of Eden. The promised land was sacred space where God's image bearers were to live for his glory and delight in his laws as they shined the light of the knowledge of God to the nations.

The conquest of the land was the exercise of dominion over idolatry and wickedness so that the right worship of the true and living God would flourish and increase.

THE LAND AND A FUTURE JOSHUA

The land of promise remained important for the rest of the Old Testament. Kings reigned and prophets ministered there. The Israelites would eventually be exiled from and then restored to it.

In the New Testament, the context of Jesus' public ministry is this same land. The beginning of his ministry is associated with his baptism by John the Baptist, which took place in the Jordan River (Matt. 3:13–17). By going into the waters of the Jordan, Jesus is Israel preparing for conquest.

Understanding Jesus' ministry as a conquest is appropriate. His name, after all, is "Jesus," which is the Greek equivalent of the Hebrew name "Joshua," meaning "Yahweh is salvation." He is a new and greater Joshua, and he traveled into the northern and southern parts of the land exercising dominion. Rather than facing the armies of Jericho or Ai, Jesus subdued blindness, deafness, paralysis, and death. Jesus filled the promised land with the signs of salvation.

THE RISE OF JUDGES

Between the conquest of the land and the establishment of Israel's monarchy, there was a period of time when everyone did what was right in their own eyes (Judg. 21:25). Joshua had died, and no one succeeded him to lead the nation.

As the years passed, the Israelites began imitating the idolaters who remained in the land. The Israelites served the gods of the nations (Judg. 2:11–13). So the Lord raised up adversaries to oppose the Israelites, who then called upon God in their distress (2:14–15). In response to the distress of his people, the Lord then raised up judges to deliver the Israelites from their enemies (2:16).

The cycle continued: the Israelites sinned, the Lord caused opposition to them, the people cried out, the Lord raised up a judge, the judge delivered them, and the Israelites went wayward once again. God's people needed a king who would lead them in righteousness and seek God's heart.

During the period of the judges, the Lord was preparing such a king. Boaz, who was from Bethlehem, married a woman named Ruth, and they had a child named Obed. From Obed came Jesse, and Jesse was the father of David (Ruth 4:22).

DAVID THE KING OF ISRAEL

The first king of Israel was Saul, but, being from Benjamin's family line, he wasn't from the right tribe (see Gen. 49:10). He was also like the kings of other nations who trusted in military strength and numbers. Saul was not the kind of king the people truly needed.

The inability of Saul to deal with the Philistines set up the prominence of young David, who slew a Philistine warrior named Goliath (1 Sam. 17) and received the praise of people (18:7). David was from the tribe of Judah and from Bethlehem in particular. A prophet named Samuel had set David apart as God's chosen man to lead the nation of Israel (16:13).

David's relationship with Saul was tense and tumultuous. Saul pursued him and opposed him, yet the Lord spared David. After Saul's death, David became king over the united kingdom of Israel around 1010 BC (2 Sam. 5:4–5).

A FUTURE SON OF DAVID

The promise-making God had a word for David through a prophet named Nathan. Though David had wanted to build a house for the Lord (a temple), the Lord would build a house for him instead (a dynasty).

David learned, "When your days are over and you rest with your ancestors, I will raise up your offspring to succeed you, your own flesh and blood, and I will establish his kingdom. He is the one who will build a house for my Name, and I will establish the throne of his kingdom forever" (2 Sam. 7:12–13).

This son of David would be king forever. The promise to David was of a future Anointed One, a Messiah, whose rule would never end. The scepter of Judah's tribe (Gen. 49:10) was now linked to the house of David. The seed from Eve's line would come from a royal house.

God's promise to David was a covenant, and God fulfilled this covenant by raising up Jesus. Matthew 1:1 states that Jesus is the "son of David" that the biblical authors anticipated. Since God promised that this future ruler would reign forever, the problem of death had to be addressed as well. As the resurrected son of David, Jesus possesses an unceasing reign because he has conquered death.

A SUFFERING KING

The years of David's kingship included suffering. When you read the psalms of David, you see a king who often felt surrounded and opposed, yet he was a king who called out to God for deliverance.

David, the suffering king, was a worshiping king. The suffering king was a singing king, a praying king, and a hoping king. David's life foreshadowed the path which Jesus would walk, for Jesus—the son of David—was also a suffering king. Jesus knew what it meant to be conspired against and opposed. He knew what betrayal was like, and he knew firsthand the heart-cry for deliverance.

THE TEMPLE IN JERUSALEM

David's son Solomon succeeded him to the throne. Solomon reigned for forty years, from 970 to 930 BC. He was given great wisdom that evoked interest from beyond the promised land (1 Kgs. 3–4; 10). His reign was more peaceful than his father's. He wrote songs and proverbs, and some of his writings were preserved among the Bible's wisdom literature.

But the most important accomplishment during Solomon's kingship was the construction of the temple in Jerusalem. David had earlier brought the ark of God to that city (2 Sam. 6:17), and now Solomon endowed the place with even greater significance by building the temple.

The temple took seven years to complete (1 Kgs. 6–8). After the priests placed the ark of God in the temple and behind the veil, "the cloud filled the temple of the LORD. And the priests could not perform their service because of the cloud, for the glory of the LORD filled his temple" (8:10–11).

This new temple replaced the tabernacle, which itself had once been filled with the glory and presence of God (Ex. 40:34–35). But unlike the tabernacle, the temple would not be portable. To that holy house the Israelites would travel from all over the promised land, celebrating feasts according to their calendar and bringing their appropriate offerings.

Jerusalem became the most important city on earth because that's where the temple of God was located. Striking, then, are the words of Jesus in John 2:19: "Destroy this temple, and I will raise it again in three days." Or consider his words in Matthew 12:6: "I tell you that something greater than the temple is here."

Jesus fulfilled the tabernacle and temple because he was the place of sacrifice. He was the perfect priest. He was the unblemished offering. There was no further need for a temple when he said from the cross, "It is finished" (John 19:30). No priest of Israel could have ever said such a thing before.

THE FRACTURE OF THE KINGDOM

While Solomon's reign was filled with greatness and significance, his son Rehoboam changed things for the nation. In 930 BC, Rehoboam became king of the united land of Israel, but he provoked a rebellion among the people. The land fractured in that year because he took the advice of some younger advisors and added to the burdens of the people (1 Kgs. 12:1–14).

The land divided into a northern and southern kingdom. A man named Jeroboam became king in the north, and Rehoboam remained king in the south. Thus began the two kingdoms that faced two destructions by two different adversaries at two different times.

David had become king around 1010 BC, and now eighty years later the land was fractured. He had received a promise of a future son who would rule forever, and now his grandson was the catalyst for irreparable damage.

A house divided against itself could not stand. The fall was certain.

EXPECTING JESUS

- Jesus is a new and greater Joshua whose name means "Yahweh is salvation."

- The ministry of Jesus was a conquest subduing the principalities and powers of this age as well as the effects of sin in this world.

- Jesus is the promised Son of David who would reign forever.

- The sacrificial work of Jesus fulfilled the purpose of the Jerusalem temple, and thus he is greater than the glorious place Solomon had built.

SUGGESTED READING

- Joshua 1–11
- Judges 1–2
- 2 Samuel 5–7
- 1 Kings 1–12

5

DEATH BY DEFEAT AND EXILE

The land of Israel experienced a slow death. The fractured kingdom lasted from 930 to 586 BC. During these years, there were unrighteous kings, corrupt priests, and pagan practices. The Lord raised up prophets who reminded the people of God's laws and holiness. If they didn't follow God's commands, God would exile them—like he did Adam and Eve—from sacred space.

COVENANT ENFORCERS

The Israelites had said at Sinai, "Everything the LORD has said we will do" (Ex. 24:3), but the covenant people in the land were not living out those words. They followed their hearts and the gods of the nations.

The northern kingdom retained the name Israel, and the southern kingdom became known as Judah. The Lord sent prophets to each of these kingdoms, that they might proclaim the promises and warnings of the Sinai covenant (see Lev. 26; Deut. 28).

The prophets were covenant enforcers.[2] They held up the commands of God like a mirror for the people. Prophets in the northern kingdom included Elijah, Elisha, Hosea, Amos, and Jonah. Prophets in the southern kingdom included Isaiah, Jeremiah, Joel, Obadiah, Micah, and Habakkuk. Some of these prophets wrote down oracles which the Spirit has preserved in the Old Testament.

Readers might hope that the Israelites would respond to the prophets with widespread repentance and contrition. But the covenant enforcers faced opposition, revilement, and rejection. Jesus indicted his own contemporaries for having a hostile heart like their ancestors who persecuted the prophets of God (Luke 11:49–51; 13:33).

---

2 I am indebted to Peter Gentry for the phrase "covenant enforcers."

The rejection of God's prophets was rooted in the people's rebellion against God. The Mosaic covenant—established in 1446 BC at Sinai—was not a refuge for sinners. The nation in the promised land had breached this covenant, and its curses would fall. The Israelites needed a new covenant and a new king, realities which Jesus would bring.

THE EMBRACE OF IDOLATRY

The level of depravity in the northern kingdom was truly shocking. After Jeroboam became its king in 930 BC, he built places of false worship in the north so that worshipers didn't have to travel to the Jerusalem temple in the south (1 Kgs. 12:26–29).

The idolatrous rituals needed a priesthood, so Jeroboam appointed priests who were not from the tribe of Levi (1 Kgs. 12:31). He even instituted a feast for the people so that they would go to the altar of idols and make offerings (12:33).

False worship and false priests coincided with a false kingship. The rulers in the north were from different dynasties, none of them from the house of David. There were approximately twenty rulers in the north before it was destroyed, and they were unrighteous kings. The institutions in the northern kingdom were illegitimate and unsanctioned.

The southern kingdom (Judah) had approximately twenty rulers as well during its years. The capital was Jerusalem where the true temple was, but that fact didn't deter all the citizens from pagan worship. The Israelites fell into idolatry, and most of their Davidic kings (the rulers descending from David's family line) were unrighteous and evil.

THE FALL OF THE NORTHERN KINGDOM

In 722 BC, the Lord raised up the Assyrian army to conquer the northern kingdom of Israel. Hoshea was the last ruler in the north, for during his reign:

> . . . the king of Assyria captured Samaria and deported the Israelites to Assyria. He settled them in Halah, in Gozan on the Habor River and in the towns of the Medes. All this took place because the Israelites had sinned against the LORD their God, who had brought them up out of Egypt from under the power of Pharaoh

king of Egypt. They worshiped other gods
(2 Kgs. 17:6–7).

The biblical author ties the defeat of the north to their transgression against the Lord. While the Lord had brought the Israelites out of captivity (Ex. 12), they were now returning to captivity! Assyria was the new Egypt. Hosea had prophesied, "Will they not return to Egypt and will not Assyria rule over them because they refuse to repent?" (Hos. 11:5). The Lord had sent prophets to warn the people, but the people refused to listen to them (2 Kgs. 17:13–15).

Taken from the sacred land, many Israelites in the north were carried east into exile. Some Israelites remained in the north and intermarried with Assyrians. The northern kingdom had lasted from 930 to 722 BC. God's judgment was unfolding, and the southern kingdom would be next.

THE FALL OF THE SOUTHERN KINGDOM

The downfall of Judah was slower. The Assyrians were not the appointed adversary for the southern kingdom, because the Babylonians conquered the Assyrian army in 612 BC. Instead, the Lord raised up the godless Babylonians to destroy the southern kingdom of Judah.

Nebuchadnezzar, the king of Babylon, came against the southern kingdom in approximately 605 BC. Some inhabitants of the land who met specific criteria (like being young and being from families of nobility) were exiled, including Daniel, Shadrach, Meshach, and Abednego (Dan. 1:3–7). In approximately 597 BC, even more people were sent into exile, including Ezekiel (Ezek. 1:1–3).

The defeat of Jerusalem came in 586 BC. Zedekiah was the last king of Judah when "Nebuchadnezzar king of Babylon marched against Jerusalem with his whole army. He encamped outside the city and built siege works all around it" (2 Kgs. 25:1). King Zedekiah was overthrown. The army set fire to the king's palace, destroyed the temple, and took the inhabitants of Judah into exile.

The southern kingdom of Judah lasted from 930 to 586 BC. God poured upon them the judgment he had promised. The holy city and its holy temple were in ruins.

THE DEATH OF THE NATION

Exiled from the promised land, the captives went east to Babylon. The exile was the death of the nation. With no king, temple, and land, the things that set apart Israel had been taken from them by Babylon—and ultimately by God.

The author of Lamentations gives insight into the devastation of Jerusalem. "How deserted lies the city, once so full of people! How like a widow is she, who once was great among the nations! She who was queen among the provinces has now become a slave" (Lam. 1:1). And, "Judah has gone into exile. She dwells among the nations; she finds no resting place. All who pursue her have overtaken her in the midst of her distress" (1:3).

Since the Israelites crossed the Jordan River around 1406 BC to inherit the promised land, their exile in 586 BC meant that they had been in the land for 820 years. Now God vomited them out, putting them outside the camp. They were an unclean people, so they went to an unclean place. They had wanted to follow the ways of the nations, so God gave them over to their desires.

QUESTIONING THE COVENANTS

In the covenant with Abraham, God had promised him many offspring that would dwell in the land of Canaan (Gen. 15:5, 18–21). The exile seemed to call this promise into question. In the covenant with David, God had promised that a future son of David would reign forever (2 Sam. 7:12–13). The deposing of the Davidic king and the destruction of the palace and city seemed to call this promise into question.

In Psalm 89, the psalmist voiced the concerns that others would have shared during the exile: "But you have rejected, you have spurned, you have been very angry with your anointed one. You have renounced the covenant with your servant and have defiled his crown in the dust. You have broken through all his walls and reduced his strongholds to ruins" (Ps. 89:38–40).

From one perspective, God's judgment on the Israelites looked like the rejection of his covenant promises. It looked like he had abandoned his people and violated his oaths.

Their redeemer had become their judge. Being slow to anger didn't mean being void of anger. The Israelites had pursued idolatry as if it was harmless. They had rejected God's law as if they wouldn't reap what they sowed.

EXPECTING JESUS

- The Israelites needed a new covenant, which Jesus would establish, for the old covenant from Sinai provided no salvation for sinners.

- Though the Davidic covenant seemed to collapse at the exile of Judah, it would be raised, confirmed, and fulfilled in the person and work of Jesus Christ.

- The unfaithfulness of Israelites in the Old Testament is an important backdrop to the faithfulness and righteousness of Jesus.

- The exile of the Israelites pointed to the deeper alienation caused by sin, and deliverance from sin would come through Christ Jesus alone.

SUGGESTED READING

- Deuteronomy 28
- 2 Kings 17–25
- Lamentations 1–5
- Psalm 89

6

HOPE IN THE DARK

The people of Israel went into exile and captivity, but the Lord went with them. Exiles needed to trust the words of the prophets that gave hope. Weeping would last for a season, but a morning of joy was on the horizon. For the time being, the Israelites needed to submit to God's hand of judgment. Their defeat was not his defeat.

FAITHFULNESS IN EXILE

There were Israelites like Jeremiah who didn't get sent to Babylon, and there were Israelites like Ezekiel and Daniel who did. Even while the nation was under God's judgment, the requirement was the same, wherever one lived: follow the Lord; trust his word; keep his commandments.

Daniel was taken as a young man to Babylon (Dan. 1:1–7), and he grew up in exile during the decades which followed. He was an example of an exiled Israelite who walked faithfully with the Lord. In the book that bears his name, we read stories of his courage, obedience, wisdom, and vindication (see Dan. 1–2; 6).

Jeremiah wrote to the exiles and gave them a word from the Lord:

> *Build houses and settle down; plant gardens and eat what they produce. Marry and have sons and daughters; find wives for your sons and give your daughters in marriage, so that they too may have sons and daughters. Increase in number there; do not decrease. Also, seek the peace and prosperity of the city to which I have carried you into exile. Pray to the LORD for it, because if it prospers, you too will prosper (Jer. 29:5–7).*

While living in exile, the Israelites were to be fruitful and multiply as they trusted the Lord and kept his commands.

SEVENTY YEARS OF CAPTIVITY

In Jeremiah's words for the captives, he wrote, "This is what the LORD says: 'When seventy years are completed for Babylon, I will come to you and fulfill my good promise to bring you back to this place'" (Jer. 29:10). This seventy-year judgment was noted by Daniel. He wrote, "I, Daniel, understood from the Scriptures, according to the word of the LORD given to Jeremiah the prophet, that the desolation of Jerusalem would last seventy years" (Dan. 9:2).[3]

Back when Solomon dedicated the temple in Jerusalem, he prayed words that considered the possibility of Israel's future disobedience and exile. And yet Solomon knew that such judgment wasn't necessarily permanent. If the Israelites would humble themselves and pray, "then from heaven, your dwelling place, hear their prayer and their plea, and uphold their cause. And forgive your people, who have sinned against you; forgive all the offenses they have committed against you, and cause their captors to show them mercy" (1 Kgs. 8:49–50).

---

3 The number "seventy" may be more of a round number than an exact one. Since 70 is the product of 7 x 10, it may symbolize a fitting and thorough judgment.

Though the Israelites had broken their covenant with God, and though they had faced the curse of exile, hope was not lost. Their temporary judgment was part of a larger plan that included regathering and restoration.

THE HOPE FOR RESTORATION

The coming release from captivity would mean restoration. Jeremiah wrote to the exiles,

> *"You will seek me and find me when you seek me with all your heart. I will be found by you," declares the LORD, "and will bring you back from captivity. I will gather you from all the nations and places where I have banished you," declares the LORD, "and will bring you back to the place from which I carried you into exile" (Jer. 29:13–14).*

If the exile to Babylon was the death of Israel, then their return would be like a resurrection from the dead. This reality is what Ezekiel saw in a vision. In a valley of dry bones, he heard the Lord say,

Son of man, these bones are the people of Israel. They say, "Our bones are dried up and our hope is gone; we are cut off." Therefore prophesy and say to them: "This is what the Sovereign Lord says: My people, I am going to open your graves and bring you up from them; I will bring you back to the land of Israel" (Ezek. 37:11–12).

The deliverance of the Israelites would be a new exodus. Yahweh is the God of the exodus and Red Sea crossing (Isa. 43:2, 16–17). God will demonstrate his love to his people, and they shall pass through a door of hope (Hos. 2:14–15).

A NEW DAVID

A restored people would need a king, so the prophets spoke of one to come. Not just any king would do. The Israelites would need a new David to reign over them. This expectation stemmed from God's commitment to his covenant in 2 Samuel 7:12–13.

God said to Ezekiel, "My servant David will be king over them, and they will all have one shepherd. They will follow my laws and be careful to keep my decrees" (Ezek. 37:24). This prophecy anticipated a unified people, not a fractured nation. And since this Davidic hope was not about a reincarnate David, the wording recalled the covenant in 2 Samuel 7.

There would be a new David, a son of David, who would be the shepherd that the people needed. This shepherd-king would reign forever. His coming would bring dominion, and his dominion would not end. This vast and glorious kingdom is what Daniel described when he recounted Nebuchadnezzar's dream: "In the time of those kings, the God of heaven will set up a kingdom that will never be destroyed, nor will it be left to another people. It will crush all those kingdoms and bring them to an end, but it will itself endure forever" (Dan. 2:44).

The new king's arrival would be dawn in the darkness (Isa. 9:2). Isaiah prophesied of that day: "For to us a child is born, to us a son is given, and the government will be on his shoulders. And he will be called Wonderful Counselor, Mighty God, Everlasting Father, Prince of Peace" (9:6). This son would establish the throne of David forever (9:7).

Jesus was the new David, and by his death and resurrection he has secured the throne. His coming brought light to the darkness (John 8:12). He was the heavenly Stone that came to subdue and to extend dominion (Dan. 2:34, 44).

As the Israelites dwelled in exile and needed hope, the prophets told not only of their near restoration to the land but also of a deliverer. The Messiah, the long-awaited son of Eve, would rule with righteousness.

A NEW COVENANT

The prophets gave their audience hope for a relationship with God that transcended the old covenant. Something new was coming.

Under the old covenant made at Sinai, the Israelites faced curse and exile, death and destruction. But in Jeremiah's oracles we read,

> *"The days are coming," declares the LORD, "when I will make a new covenant with the people of Israel and with the people of Judah. It will not be like the covenant I made with their ancestors when I took them by the hand to lead them out of Egypt, because they broke my covenant, though I was a husband to them,"*

declares the LORD. *"This is the covenant I will make with the people of Israel after that time," declares the* LORD. *"I will put my law in their minds and write it on their hearts. I will be their God, and they will be my people. No longer will they teach their neighbor, or say to one another, 'Know the* LORD,' *because they will all know me, from the least of them to the greatest," declares the* LORD. *"For I will forgive their wickedness and will remember their sins no more" (Jer. 31:31–34).*

Other prophets spoke of this future covenant, though they didn't use the word "new" like Jeremiah's prophecy did. Their promises are still parallel to his. For example, in Ezekiel 36, the Lord says to Ezekiel, "I will give you a new heart and put a new spirit in you; I will remove from you your heart of stone and give you a heart of flesh. And I will put my Spirit in you and move you to follow my decrees and be careful to keep my laws" (Ezek. 36:26–27). And in Daniel's prophecy, a future Anointed One would make a "covenant" (Dan. 9:27).

This new covenant was what Jesus established by his body and blood (see Luke 22:20). Through faith in Christ, sinners would be joined to their Savior in an unbreakable union, a covenant sealed by his perfect work on the cross. Through a new exodus, the new David would form a new covenant.

THE FALL OF BABYLON

The Babylonian captors would not rule over the Israelites forever. God had foretold the fall of their empire (Jer. 51; Dan. 2:37–39). He is sovereign over kings and kingdoms, and he would demonstrate this truth by humbling the self-exalting Babylonians.

Israel's exile came to an end in 539 BC. The Babylonian officials were in the middle of a banquet, at King Belshazzar's arrangement, when an ominous hand appeared and wrote words of judgment on the wall (Dan. 5:5, 24–28). Mighty Babylon fell that night to the Medo-Persian Empire, led by Cyrus the Persian.

The words of Jeremiah 51:10 had come true at last: "The LORD has vindicated us; come, let us tell in Zion what the LORD our God has done."

EXPECTING JESUS

- Jesus would be the shepherd-king to gather and guide the people of God.

- The death of Jesus on the cross established, through his body and blood, the new covenant which the Old Testament had promised.

- The saving work of Jesus was a new exodus movement leading sinners away from their captivity to sin, Satan, and death.

- The coming of Jesus fulfilled the promise of a king and kingdom that would never end.

SUGGESTED READING

- 1 Kings 8:22–53

- Jeremiah 29:1–23

- Daniel 2

- Ezekiel 37

7

GOING BACK AND GOING UP

With the Babylonian army overcome, Cyrus the Persian made a proclamation: "The LORD, the God of heaven, has given me all the kingdoms of the earth and he has appointed me to build a temple for him at Jerusalem in Judah. Any of his people among you may go up, and may the LORD their God be with them" (2 Chr. 36:23).

THE FIRST RETURN

When the Medo-Persians defeated the Babylonians in 539 BC, King Cyrus permitted the Israelites to return to the promised land. The first return was in the next few years, in approximately 536 BC, led by a man named Zerubbabel (Ezra 1–2).

More than 50,000 Israelites returned to the promised land, leaving their life of exile in the land of Babylon. But many more thousands of Israelites remained dispersed. Perhaps Bible readers would have imagined that all the Israelites would be eager to flee Babylon, just as they fled Egypt in 1446 BC under Moses' leadership. Yet most of the Israelites who had been exiled by Babylon remained outside the promised land. Had their zeal for the promised land waned? Had they become complacent?

The returnees, however, had a job to do: to renew life in this sacred space. They focused on laying the foundation of the temple and rebuilding the altar (Ezra 3). The rebuilding of the mighty temple had begun! This task was key to their lives as Israelites, because the presence of the temple set Jerusalem apart as a holy city. The temple was the dwelling place of God's manifest glory from the days of Solomon to its destruction.

UNFINISHED TASKS

As time passed, the rebuilding slowed. Eventually the rebuilding of the temple ceased altogether. The Israelites had become discouraged, and they focused instead on building their own homes. The neglect of God's house was obvious. This oversight was a spiritual problem. What did it say about the former exiles if they had returned to the land but let the temple remain in ruins?

In 520 BC, the Lord raised up Haggai and Zechariah to confront the lethargy of the Jews in the land. Haggai gave a word from God:

> Is it a time for you yourselves to be living in your paneled houses, while this house remains a ruin? Now this is what the LORD Almighty says: "Give careful thought to your ways. You have planted much, but harvested little. You eat, but never have enough. You drink, but never have your fill. You put on clothes, but are not warm. You earn wages, only to put them in a purse with holes in it" (Hag. 1:4–6).

The words of God, through the prophet Haggai, rebuked the people for ignoring the unfinished temple. The Israelites had been experiencing agricultural difficulties in the land. Their unfaithfulness had been costly. Their agricultural problems were signs of spiritual complacency and compromise.

THE REBUILT TEMPLE

The ministries of Haggai and Zechariah were effective. The people renewed their labor and completed the rebuilt temple in approximately 516 BC. Though the temple under Solomon took only seven years to build (1 Kgs. 5–8), this rebuilt temple under Zerubbabel was completed after twenty years of the returnees being back in the land.

But something was missing. After the exodus from Egypt, when the Israelites set up the tabernacle, the glory of the Lord filled it (Ex. 40:34). And when the temple was completed during Solomon's reign, the glory of the Lord filled it too (1 Kgs. 8:11). But there is no report of glory filling the rebuilt temple in the days of Zerubbabel.

When the Babylonians carried off the Jerusalem temple's vessels to the east (Dan. 1:2), the ark of God went into exile in their hands. And this ark was never recovered. The Israelites did not reinstall the ark of the covenant into the rebuilt temple.

In the book of Haggai, the prophet asked Judah's governor (Zerubbabel) and the high priest (Joshua), "Who of you is left who saw this house in its former glory? How does it look to you now? Does it not seem to you like nothing?" (Hag. 2:3).

Compared to its predecessor, the rebuilt temple was a disappointment. It lacked the glory and majesty of Solomon's temple. Yet Haggai gave a word from the Lord: "'The glory of this present house will be greater than the glory of the former house,' says the Lord Almighty. 'And in this place I will grant peace,' declares the Lord Almighty" (Hag. 2:9).

The rebuilt temple, though lacking glory, would one day give way to greater glory. There was hope for a surpassingly great temple. That day came when Jesus was born and tabernacled (dwelt) among sinners (John 1:14). His body was the holy place that would be torn down and rebuilt—torn down by death and rebuilt by resurrection (2:20–22).

This rebuilt temple from the days of Zerubbabel was still standing in the days of Jesus. When he said, "I tell you that something greater than the temple is here" (Matt. 12:6), he was talking about himself.

THE STORY OF ESTHER

Since many Israelites stayed dispersed outside the promised land, it's not a surprise to the Bible reader to read a story of Jews in Persia. The story in the book of Esther took place from about 483 to 473 BC. During these ten years, a Jewish woman named Esther became queen when she married King Xerxes.

A threat arose against the Jewish people through a villain named Haman, and Esther was in the right place at the right time to intervene on behalf of the Jewish people (Esth. 4–7). The deliverance of the Jewish people was important because Persia had charge of the promised land. If Jews died throughout the Persian Empire, that threatened the lives of Jews in the promised land as well.

God's providential work through Esther showed his covenant faithfulness. Though the seed of the serpent threatened the seed of the woman, God gave victory to his people (Esth. 8–9), thus preserving the messianic hope.

THE ARRIVAL OF EZRA

The Israelites in the promised land needed help. They needed spiritual instruction. Though they were no longer in Babylonian captivity, there was a deeper, inward exile that characterized them. In 458 BC, a priest named Ezra traveled to the promised land, and to Jerusalem, to help them (Ezra 7:1–6).

When Ezra arrived, he encountered a people who needed to be taught. There was a need for Levites, so he called for them to return too (Ezra 8). Some Israelites had intermarried with idolaters, so the ministry of Ezra involved addressing the spiritual corruption in the hearts of people.

While a political deliverer had freed the Israelites from captivity, they needed a spiritual deliverer to free them from a greater bondage. They needed a new David who could form a new covenant for a new people.

NEHEMIAH AND THE WALL

Before the destruction of Jerusalem in 586 BC, the city was surrounded by a wall. The wall's destruction had shown the ruin of Zion for decades. And in the days of Ezra, the Jerusalem wall was still unfinished.

This unfinished wall symbolized the reality of a spiritual problem in the hearts of the Israelites.

The people were unfinished; they were in spiritual ruins. They needed renewal and revival. And to symbolize the rebuilding of the people, the wall needed rebuilding as well.

Nehemiah was a cupbearer in Persia, but he left the Persian administration (with the king's blessing) to travel to Jerusalem in 445 BC. He led the rebuilding of the wall around Jerusalem (Neh. 1–3). Though he and his team faced discouragement and hostility during the rebuilding process (4–6), they completed the wall in fifty-two days in 444 BC (6:15).

With a rebuilt temple and a rebuilt wall, the city of Jerusalem more closely resembled pre-exile times. Yet the spiritual condition of the Israelites remained a concern. It had taken nearly twenty years to rebuild the temple, and the wall was rebuilt almost one hundred years after the first group of exiles returned to the promised land.

The complacency in the people's hearts and the spiritual neglect in their lives further demonstrated the need for a deliverer. They needed more than a new temple and a new wall. They needed new hearts and new birth.

EXPECTING JESUS

- The abiding spiritual condition of the Israelites couldn't be fixed by a physical return from exile; the new covenant work of Jesus Christ was the remedy.

- Jesus is the true temple that was destroyed by death and rebuilt by resurrection.

- The book of Esther tells the triumph of the seed of the woman over the seed of the serpent, and this victory points to the ultimate triumph which Jesus would have through his work on the cross.

- The continued sin and corruption of the people of Israel gave further evidence of a need for a new covenant in which they would be forever secure and blessed, a new covenant which Jesus would make.

SUGGESTED READING

- Haggai 1–2
- Esther 1–7
- Ezra 7–10
- Nehemiah 1–6

8

LOOKING FOR AN ENDING

There was no king in Israel, and everyone did what was right in their own eyes. Life in the promised land had not yet matched the prophecies that the people had heard. The Jews lacked the spiritual fervor and devotion that ought to have marked an exodus people.

THE PROPHET MALACHI

In the 400s BC, during the years overlapping with Ezra and Nehemiah, the prophet Malachi ministered in the southern part of the promised land. He confronted a people whose hearts were wayward, for their spiritual problems were manifold.

The Israelites spoke as if God hadn't shown them steadfast love (Mal. 1:2–3). They polluted the altar by bringing inappropriate offerings (1:7–8). The priests were corrupt and ignored the criteria for proper sacrificial offerings (2:1–9). There were Israelites who married idolaters (2:10–16). Some people claimed that God didn't care about what was just (2:17). Truly a blindness and hardness of heart had settled over the people.

Through Malachi, the Lord warned his people about judgment (Mal. 3:1–3, 9; 4:3). The wicked would perish, but the people of God had a different future: "for you who revere my name, the sun of righteousness will rise with healing in its rays. And you will go out and frolic like well-fed calves" (4:2).

NOT LIKE IT WAS

Life in the promised land was a shadow of its former glory. The temple had been rebuilt, but it was less glorious than the one built under Solomon's kingship. The wall around Jerusalem had been restored, but only after the people had neglected it for nearly a hundred years. With corrupt people and priests, life in the promised land did not usher in a golden age of worship and flourishing.

Persia was the ruling power. While the Israelites could return to Jerusalem, they couldn't install the next son of David on the throne as king. They were a ruled people now. The king of Persia was king over the promised land. The Messiah had not come, and the house of David hadn't been raised from the ruins.

The Old Testament era ends with a sense of incompleteness. The Old Testament story is an incomplete story.

400 YEARS OF SILENCE

Malachi was the final Old Testament prophet, and then the prophetic voice went silent. A series of centuries had no word from the Lord. These years are sometimes called the "four hundred years of silence." But this lengthy time was hardly silent when it came to social and political events, though the Lord didn't raise up another prophet.

The intertestamental era—the four hundred years between the Old and New Testaments—was eventful. The Persians fell to the Greeks in 331 BC. Alexander the Great led the Greek army, and this victory ushered in Greek rule over the promised land. This event fulfilled Daniel's earlier prophecy that the Greeks would defeat the Persians (Dan. 8:20–21).

After Alexander the Great died, his kingdom was divided among military leaders. One of these leaders, named Seleucus, ruled north of the promised land, and his successors posed threats to the Israelites. One Seleucid king in particular, Antiochus IV, was a diabolical figure who inflicted terrible hardships and persecution upon the Israelites in Jerusalem. From 167 to 164 BC, the Israelites endured the king's tyrannical ways, until eventually the Maccabees helped to secure the temple and rededicate it for right worship.

In 146 BC, the Romans rose against the Greeks and defeated them at Corinth. The dominion of Rome would eventually encompass the promised land. The Roman Empire was the fourth kingdom which Daniel spoke about (Dan. 2:40–45), and it would be the political context for the first advent of Jesus.

HORIZONS NEAR AND FAR

The unfulfilled prophecies at the end of the Old Testament era confirm that interpreters should see the prophets as speaking on two horizons. The near horizon of their prophecies included the defeat of Babylon and the geographical return of the Israelites to the promised land.

But the far horizon of the biblical prophets incorporated the messianic hopes and "new exodus" imagery which didn't come to pass during the Old Testament era. The effects of the curse were known and felt. Injustice still existed. Death still claimed image bearers with its seemingly invincible grip. The ongoing nature of the sacrificial system showed that our sins needed full and final atonement. The whole earth had not yet been filled with the knowledge of the glory of God.

Yet if God had fulfilled what was on the prophets' near horizon, he would also accomplish what was on their far horizon. In the fullness of time, the Messiah would come to redeem and renew.

FORWARD WITH FAITH AND HOPE

In the Old Testament story line, those who loved the Lord walked by faith. After highlighting a myriad of these faithful saints, the author of Hebrews says, "These were all commended for their faith, yet none of them received what had been promised, since God had planned something better for us so that only together with us would they be made perfect" (Heb. 11:39–40).

The biblical authors were forward-looking, confident that God would work his will on earth as it is in heaven. As God promised, he would raise up the son from David's line who would rule forever in righteousness. As God promised, he would bring blessing to the families of the earth through the line of Abraham. As God promised, he would bring the son of Eve into history with a mission of victory. Hope for all the earth had been promised, and hope would come.

The Old Testament reveals the loving heart of God who pursues sinners with relentless grace. The end of the Old Testament is not the end of the Bible's story, and the heavenly silence during the intertestamental period would not last.

The angel Gabriel came to an old priest named Zechariah (Luke 1), and to a young virgin named Mary who was betrothed to a man named Joseph (Matt. 1). The silence was broken. There was good news of great joy for all people.

EXPECTING JESUS

- Though a king from David's line didn't return to the throne in Jerusalem after the exile ended, God preserved the Davidic line that led to Jesus the Son of David.

- The priesthood in the days of Malachi was corrupt, but the ministry and death of Jesus would be the work of a perfect and faithful priest whose offering and intercession would accomplish atonement.

- Four hundred years of prophetic silence began after Malachi's ministry, but the silence was broken when the time of the Messiah had finally come.

- The non-glorious and incomplete ending of the Old Testament story line sets up the joyous fulfillment of its promises and hopes in the ministry of Jesus Christ.

SUGGESTED READING

- Malachi 1–4
- Isaiah 52–53
- Daniel 8
- Luke 1–2

RECOMMENDED RESOURCES

To help you approach and understand the Bible faithfully, I recommend the following resources.

T. Desmond Alexander's *From Eden to the New Jerusalem: An Introduction to Biblical Theology* (Kregel, 2009)

G. K. Beale and Mitchell Kim's *God Dwells Among Us: Expanding Eden to the Ends of the Earth* (IVP, 2014)

Mitchell Chase's *40 Questions About Typology and Allegory* (Kregel, 2020)

Stephen Dempster's *Dominion and Dynasty: A Theology of the Hebrew Bible* (IVP, 2003)

James Hamilton's *God's Glory in Salvation through Judgment: A Biblical Theology* (Crossway, 2010)

James Hamilton's *What Is Biblical Theology? A Guide to the Bible's Story, Symbolism, and Patterns* (Crossway, 2013)

L. Michael Morales's *Exodus Old and New: A Biblical Theology of Redemption* (IVP, 2020)

Thomas Schreiner's *The King in His Beauty: A Biblical Theology of the Old and New Testaments* (Baker, 2013)

Matt Smethurst's *Before You Open Your Bible: Nine Heart Postures for Approaching God's Word* (10Publishing, 2019)